DAYS OF DECISION

Kennedy and the Cuban Missile Crisis

Heinemann
LIBRARY
Chicago, Illinois

Cath Senker

© 2014 Heinemann Library
an imprint of Capstone Global Library, LLC
Chicago, Illinois

Visit our web site at www.heinemannraintree.com

Edited by Andrew Farrow, Adrian Vigliano, and Mark Friedman
Designed by Cynthia Della-Rovere
Original illustrations © Capstone Global Library Ltd.
Illustrated by H L Studios and Cynthia Della-Rovere
Picture research by Elizabeth Alexander
Production by Sophia Argyris

Originated by Capstone Global Library Ltd
Printed in China by RR Donnelley South China

17 16 15 14 13
10 9 8 7 6 5 4 3 2 1

Library of Congress Cataloging-in-Publication Data
Senker, Cath.

Kennedy and the Cuban missile crisis / Cath Senker.

pages cm.—(Days of decision)

Includes bibliographical references and index.

ISBN 978-1-4329-7637-8 (hb)—ISBN 978-1-4329-7644-6 (pb) 1. Cuban Missile Crisis, 1962—Juvenile literature. 2. Kennedy, John F. (John Fitzgerald), 1917-1963—Juvenile literature. I. Title.

E841.S46 2013

973.922092—dc23   2012041747

Acknowledgments
The author and publishers are grateful to the following for permission to reproduce copyright material: ©Corbis pp. 7, 47; Alamy p. 52 (©Chris Hammond); Corbis pp. 4, 15, 21, 23, 25, 27, 28, 37, 45, 48 (©Bettmann), 53 (©Hulton-Deutsch Collection); Gamma-Rapho via Getty Images imprint page (Carl Steffen); Getty Images pp. 8 (Hulton Archive), 16 (Three Lions/Hulton Archive), 29 (Keystone/Hulton Archive), 30 (Carl Mydans/Time & Life Pictures), 34 (Time & Life Pictures/ Francis Miller); Photoshot pp. 6 (©UPPA), 12 (©WpN), 39 (Alexei Stuzhin), 50 (©UPPA); Press Association Images p. 41 (AP Photo); Rex p. 42 (White House); Robert Knudsen, White House/ John F. Kennedy Presidential Library and Museum, Boston p. 10.

Background and design features reproduced with the permission of Shutterstock (©Picsfive, ©Petrov Stanislav, ©Zastolskiy Victor, ©design36, ©a454).

Cover photograph of Kennedy giving a speech at Rice University reproduced with the permission of Superstock (NASA/Science Faction); Cover photograph of an American Navy ship alongside a Soviet freighter reproduced with the permission of Getty Images (Popperfoto).

We would like to thank Dr. John Allen Williams for his invaluable help in the preparation of this book.

Every effort has been made to contact copyright holders of any material reproduced in this book. Any omissions will be rectified in subsequent printings if notice is given to the publisher.

Contents

Some words are printed in **bold**, like this. You can find out what they mean by looking in the glossary on page 60.

On the Brink of Nuclear War

It is October 27, 1962, and the middle of the Cuban Missile Crisis. At this moment, **nuclear** war could become a reality. Only twice has a country ever used nuclear weapons. In August 1945, U.S. forces dropped nuclear weapons on the Japanese cities of Hiroshima and Nagasaki, killing more than 100,000 people instantly and devastating everything in the area.[1] The world feared a similar catastrophe.

Now, in 1962, the United States and its enemy, the **Soviet Union** (also called the Union of Soviet Socialist Republics, or USSR), are head-to-head. The Soviet Union has nuclear missiles located on Cuba, a Caribbean island just 90 miles (140 kilometers) from the United States. U.S. forces are on high alert around the Caribbean,

In grave danger

A high school student in Canada explained how it felt during the Cuban Missile Crisis of 1962:

"For several days everyone at my high school thought of nothing else. We were convinced we were going to die a horrible nuclear death at any moment because Halifax, Nova Scotia, a major seaport and naval base, would have been a bull's-eye of a first strike target. They told us we would have a 20-minute warning. Twenty minutes to live, once the sirens sounded.

Naturally everyone talked about what they would do with those last 20 minutes of life. Knowing for certain we would all die, most planned to do things they would normally never have done."[3]

In the United States, students in the early 1960s learned to protect themselves in the event of a nuclear attack by ducking under their desks.

ready to launch a military strike at a moment's notice. Such an attack would risk nuclear **retaliation**.

Looking back, US President John F. Kennedy's aide (assistant) Arthur Schlesinger remembered, "It was the most dangerous moment in human history."[2]

Immediate threat

During the 1950s and 1960s, people living within range of the **Soviet** missiles were genuinely fearful that nuclear war would happen at any time. They learned to be prepared. In the United States, a cartoon figure called Bert the Turtle told viewers that if they heard an air-raid siren, they should "duck and cover," seeking shelter under a table or other item of heavy furniture. In school, children practiced emergency drills, taking cover under their desks when the alarm sounded.

The United States' concerns about communism

The following extract is from a U.S. Secretary of Defense booklet about the Cuba situation, dated October 29, 1962. It explains why the U.S. government was so angry about the missiles in Cuba:

"The United States and its **Allies** are responding to a sudden, sinister threat to world peace and security. The USSR [Soviet Union] has attempted to upset the delicate balance of world power by secretly introducing its **offensive weapons** into the Western Hemisphere, using Cuba as a strategic base…

Why is America, the richest and strongest nation in the world, worrying about Communism in Cuba?

Because once a country falls under the control of **Communists** its government becomes subject to control by the Kremlin [Soviet government], and an instrument for the aggressive Communist world movement."[4]

Day of decision

In late October 1962, in this tense atmosphere, President Kennedy needed to decide what to do about the Soviets and Cuba. At the time, there was a great deal of pressure for US leaders to stand up to the political philosophy of **communism**, which the Soviet Union followed. (For more on the two countries' conflicting beliefs, see page 9.) Should Kennedy negotiate with the Soviet Union and risk being seen as a weak leader who would not stand up to communism? Or should he risk the lives of millions of people by launching a military strike on Cuba? Kennedy faced the toughest test of his leadership.

The Making of a President

So, who was the US president making life-or-death decisions during the Cuban Missile Crisis? John F. Kennedy had become president in 1961, but he would govern for just two years before being **assassinated** in 1963.

John F. Kennedy was born in 1917 to a wealthy Irish-Catholic family, the second of nine children. John's father, Joseph P. Kennedy, was a bank president and a multimillionaire. He was also involved in shipbuilding, bootlegging (the illegal trade of alcohol), and the movie industry.[1] Joe's wealth allowed his children to live comfortably their entire lives.[2] John's mother, Rose, was the daughter of John F. Fitzgerald, who was the mayor of Boston from 1906 to 1907.

John was frequently sick. As an adult, he would be diagnosed with Addison's disease, which causes serious stomach problems. Yet John was determined not to allow his health problems to affect his life and career.

A published author

In 1936, John went to Harvard University. The following year, his father was called US **ambassador** to Great Britain, and so most of the family moved to England. Starting in 1938, John served as his father's secretary, taking the opportunity to travel around Europe and gather information for his college **thesis**.

Joseph P. Kennedy in his role as U.S. ambassador to Britain, on his arrival in Southampton, England, in July 1938. He is with his sons John (right) and Joseph, Jr.

Following the outbreak of World War II (1939–1945), John published his thesis as a book, *Why England Slept* (1940).[3] It focused on Britain's failure to prepare for war and argued for a firm response to **Nazi** Germany. John himself participated in the war effort, joining the US Navy and going to sea in 1942. His oldest brother, Joe, Jr., was killed fighting with the US Navy.

Into politics

After the war ended in 1945, John chose to enter politics, running for the US Congress as a **Democrat**. His grandfather had been a congressman and his father had been an ambassador, so the Kennedys had considerable political influence. The family provided financial backing, and the Kennedy women held magnificent tea parties to attract support. These grand social occasions attracted many influential people.[4]

In 1946, at the age of 29, John F. Kennedy was elected. He served as a congressman in the House of Representatives from 1947 to 1953. During his time there, he called for better conditions for working people, lower rents, and improved **social security** payments for the elderly.[5]

A young hero

In 1943, John F. Kennedy became captain of a patrol **torpedo** (PT) boat. The small craft was rammed by a Japanese destroyer (a fast warship) and was ripped apart. John led his men to safety by swimming to a nearby island and managed to communicate with local people to get help. He and his crew were rescued. John was later awarded medals for heroism and injuries suffered while serving his country.[6]

John F. Kennedy in his patrol torpedo boat, while serving in the U.S. Navy in the early 1940s. He served in the navy from fall 1941 to 1945.

Early years in government

John F. Kennedy was an ambitious young man, eager to further his career in politics. With his brother Robert (known as Bobby) managing his campaign and additional "Kennedy teas" provided by his mother and sisters, he was elected to the US Senate in 1952.[7]

Kennedy's early years in government came at a time of great upheaval in the United States. Since the late 1940s, the African-American struggle for **civil rights** had been a major issue in **domestic** politics. In 1954, a key Supreme Court ruling established that **segregation** was illegal in US schools. Kennedy agreed that African Americans should have the same civil rights as white Americans.

The civil rights movement

In the United States after World War II, African Americans were still being treated as second-class citizens. They were separated from white people in schools, public restrooms, public transportation, and other public areas. Conditions were particularly harsh in the South, where African Americans who attempted to exert their civil rights were frequently attacked or even murdered.

In the 1950s, the civil rights movement arose to challenge this injustice, focusing first on segregation in public schools. The movement adopted a range of tactics, including legal action, marches, boycotts (refusing to buy products or use services), public protests, and civil disobedience (disobeying rules as a form of peaceful protest).[8]

The fear of communism

In foreign policy, the US government was working to persuade other countries to become allies with the United States. In particular, it was pursuing countries that, like the United States, were **democracies** and had economies based on **capitalism**–not communism, like the Soviet Union. These tensions were known as the **Cold War** (see the box).

Many Americans feared that communists might take over the government of their country, and they were suspicious that people around them might be communist sympathizers. Kennedy also believed it was important to resist communism.

In 1958, Kennedy was re-elected to the Senate, with the largest majority of any senatorial candidate that year.[9] He became determined to win the top job–the presidency.

The Cold War

During the Cold War (late 1940s to 1990), large areas of the world were divided into hostile groups led by the two **superpowers**: the United States and the Soviet Union.

The United States and its Western European allies were mostly democracies where people voted for their government representatives. Their economic system was capitalism—private companies carried out most production and trade.

The Soviet Union led the other alliance. It included the Eastern European and Central Asian states, where Soviet influence was strong. These countries had communist governments run by a single, unelected party—the Communist Party. The state owned and ran industries and agriculture (farming). China was also a communist country.

The war was called a "Cold War" because there was no fighting directly between the superpowers. Yet when there was a conflict in the world, the United States and the Soviet Union took sides and provided weapons to their allies. For example, a war in Laos (in Southeast Asia) took place between forces supported by the communists and opponents backed by the United States (see pages 20 and 21). Both superpowers possessed nuclear weapons, claiming that these powerful weapons were necessary for defense. When the United States and Soviet Union came close to starting a real conflict, the world faced the terrifying prospect of nuclear war.

The top job

During the 1960 campaign for the presidency, Kennedy presented himself as the new, young face of the modern United States, in opposition to the experienced **Republican** candidate, Richard Nixon. Kennedy campaigned around the country, introducing his **"New Frontier"** program, which aimed to tackle the problems of poverty and racial prejudice, while also exploring space and new areas of science.

Kennedy faced several obstacles in being elected president. He was young, he was a Catholic (a minority faith in the United States), and he had never served as a senior member of government. But the American people decided that the time for the New Frontier had arrived, and they elected Kennedy. He and his wife, Jacqueline (known

John and Jackie Kennedy with violinist Isaac Stern at a dinner in the White House for a French minister in May 1962.

Jacqueline (Jackie) Kennedy Onassis 1929–1994

Born: Southampton, New York

Role: First lady, 1961–1963; wife of John F. Kennedy

Jacqueline Bouvier married John F. Kennedy in 1953 and became one of the most popular first ladies in U.S. history. She refurbished the White House with valuable art and furniture and invited well-known actors, artists, and intellectuals to visit. As a fluent French speaker with excellent fashion sense, Jackie was warmly welcomed when the Kennedys toured France in 1961. Jackie was present in the car when her husband was assassinated, and she bravely stood by incoming president Lyndon B. Johnson as he took over the presidency just an hour and a half later.

Did you know? Later, in 1968, Jackie married the Greek shipping millionaire Aristotle Onassis.[10]

as Jackie), moved their young family into the White House, and they proved enormously popular.

Reducing poverty

President Kennedy's New Frontier speeches led to great expectations of change. The new president achieved some social welfare reforms to help poor Americans: he increased social security payments and the minimum wage (the lowest amount of money people can legally be paid for work). He also increased unemployment benefits.[11] To assist people living in poverty abroad, he supported the Food for Peace Program, which donated U.S. food overseas. In 1961, Kennedy set up the Peace Corps, to send young Americans to developing countries where they could contribute their skills (see page 13).

Kennedy did not succeed in all areas. He was unable to get health insurance for the elderly or cuts in income tax passed through Congress.[12]

Civil rights: Limited reform

President Kennedy's civil rights program also fell short. He introduced some laws—for example, in March 1961, he established the President's Committee on Equal Employment Opportunity. This made it illegal to discriminate (select based on race) when hiring **federal** workers and denied federal contracts to businesses that practiced **discrimination**. In November 1962, Kennedy brought in a limited law to stop racial segregation in public housing.

The speech Kennedy delivered when he was sworn in as president in January 1961 became part of his **legacy**. The speech ended with a call for Americans to participate in their country and act as world citizens, rather than expecting their rulers to run society for them. He said:

"And so, my fellow Americans: Ask not what your country can do for you—ask what you can do for your country. My fellow citizens of the world, ask not what America will do for you, but what, together, we can do for the freedom of man."[13]

To read the speech and see a video of it, go to www.jfklibrary.org/Asset-Viewer/BqXIEM9F4024ntFI7SVAjA.aspx.

Elizabeth Eckford (front), one of a group of black students who attempted to enter Little Rock High School, Arkansas, in 1957, during the campaign to integrate education.

The New Frontier: Civil rights

The struggle for civil rights was marked by violent confrontations between civil rights activists and their opponents. President Kennedy provided some protection for protesters. In 1961, the "freedom riders" of the Congress of Racial Equality (CORE) demonstrated against racial segregation on buses in the South. Because they risked attack from pro-segregationists, Kennedy sent soldiers to protect them. Kennedy also supported African American student James Meredith in his fight for the right to gain entrance to the whites-only University of Mississippi. In October 1962, Meredith was eventually able to attend the university, with the protection of federal police.[14]

Yet the violence continued. In April 1963, police in Birmingham, Alabama, attacked African American civil rights protesters–many of them children–with police dogs and high-pressure fire hoses.[15]

President Kennedy attempted to find common ground between the protesters and segregationists. By May, he realized that discussions would not be enough to achieve significant change. Instead, wide-ranging civil rights **legislation** was required to enforce equal rights. In June, he made a forceful televised speech in favor of civil rights, and the following week he asked for support in Congress to pass laws to **integrate** public facilities, arguing: "The heart of the question is whether all Americans are to be afforded equal rights and equal opportunities, whether we are going to treat our fellow Americans as we want to be treated."[16]

The civil rights movement kept up the pressure. In August 1963, a civil rights march of over 250,000 activists, led by Reverend Martin Luther King, Jr., converged in front of the Lincoln Monument in Washington, D.C.[17]

No decisive action

Yet despite the pressure, opinions among President Kennedy's advisers remained divided over civil rights. Bobby Kennedy, his brother and the US attorney general (head of the Department of Justice), believed that the government should deliver on greater equality for African Americans. However, other advisers were concerned that efforts to pass a civil rights law might fail and damage the president's standing. As a result, there was no united government effort to push through such legislation.[18] Although Kennedy made many speeches against discrimination, ultimately his "actions did not match his words," according to some people.[19] Kennedy was unable to pass a civil rights bill.

A New Frontier: Space

President Kennedy was determined to beat the Soviet Union in the race to the Moon. On April 12, 1961, the Soviet astronaut Yuri Gagarin became the first person to circle Earth in space. On May 25, 1961, President Kennedy made a speech, saying: "I believe that this nation should commit itself to achieving the goal, before this decade is out, of landing a man on the Moon and returning him safely to Earth."[20] The following year, John Glenn became the first American to orbit Earth in a spacecraft. And Kennedy's dream did come true. The first Americans set foot on the Moon on July 20, 1969.

The Peace Corps

In March 1961, President Kennedy established the Peace Corps, with the aim of sending American volunteers with useful skills to work in developing countries. Kennedy's program proved successful and long lasting. In 1961, the first 900 volunteers served in 16 countries. By 2011, there were more than 200,000 volunteers working in 139 countries.[21]

Successes

At the same time, President Kennedy had major successes in other areas, including the space programme and the Peace Corps (see the boxes above and left).

The United States and the World, 1961–1962

As president of the United States, John F. Kennedy was faced with the dilemma of how to respond to the spread of communism. Crises in Cuba, Berlin (see pages 18 and 19), and Laos (see pages 20 and 21) posed major challenges. Kennedy's experience in coping with these threats would serve him well when the Cuban Missile Crisis erupted.

Revolution in Cuba

In the years before Kennedy took office, Fulgencio Batista ruled Cuba as a dictator since 1952. Under his brutal rule, Cuba was a major producer and exporter of sugar, yet most agricultural workers barely earned enough to survive. The United States was Cuba's major trading partner, buying two-thirds of its exports in 1959.[1] The United States

Fidel Castro

Born: 1926, near Birán, Cuba

Role: Political leader of Cuba from 1959 to 2008

In the late 1950s, Fidel Castro led a revolution that forced the **regime** of Fulgencio Batista out of power. In 1959, Castro became the head of the new government. As part of his policy to improve the lives of the poor majority, he brought all businesses under state control and redistributed land from the rich to the poor. Relations with the United States worsened, while the Soviet Union became Cuba's main ally and trading partner.

Castro extended free health and education services to all Cubans and ensured that everyone had a job. However, his one-party government controlled all aspects of Cuban life. There was no freedom to criticize his policies. And due to the U.S. refusal to trade with Cuba and poor management of the economy, living standards remained generally low.[2]

After the Soviet Union collapsed in 1991, Castro allowed some free-market activity (trade that was not controlled by the government), but he maintained a tight grip on political power, denying freedom of expression. In 2008, the elderly leader handed over power to his brother Raúl.[3]

Did you know? Fidel Castro is a brilliant speaker with an incredible power to win people over.[4]

also occupied Guantánamo Bay in Cuba, which it used as a naval base. In 1959, Fidel Castro led a **revolution** in Cuba and overthrew Batista.

Castro made reforms that helped the poor and punished the rich. The government took over the mostly US-owned sugar industry, so that the income could be invested in Cuba. Many better-off Cubans fled to the US state of Florida, only 90 miles (145 kilometres) away. The United States opposed the new government in Cuba and cut off trade and **diplomatic** relations with the island.

Cuba needed new trading partners and allies. The Soviet Union began to buy Cuban sugar and other exports, and relations with this communist state began to develop. Soviet support for Cuba gave the US government serious cause for concern. Cuba had entered the Cold War.

Timeline of the widening gulf between the United States and Cuba

1960
July 5
The Cuban government takes over all U.S. property in Cuba.

1960
July 6
U.S. President Dwight D. Eisenhower (served 1953–1961) cancels Cuba's sugar quota (the fixed amount of sugar the United States purchases).

1960
August 7
Cuba takes over large U.S.-owned industrial and agricultural businesses.

1960
October 19
The United States stops most exports to Cuba.[5]

1961
January
President Eisenhower breaks off diplomatic ties with Cuba.

Fidel Castro stands above a crowd during the last days of the Cuban Revolution in 1959. Castro's movement to overthrow Batista's government had begun on July 26, 1953.

The Bay of Pigs invasion

The US **Central Intelligence Agency (CIA)** had been planning to invade Cuba and overthrow Castro since May 1960. It trained around 1,500 Cuban **exiles**. Some of them had been commanders in Batista's army.[6] The **Joint Chiefs of Staff** told Kennedy, the new president, that they were convinced that the moment these forces landed, the Cuban people would rise up alongside them to overthrow Castro. Taking their advice, Kennedy gave the go-ahead.

On April 15, 1961, US planes piloted by Cuban exiles bombed Cuban air bases. With US equipment, the exiles made their main landing in an inlet on the southern coast of Cuba known as the Bay of Pigs. The invasion was poorly planned, and it failed. The exiles were not protected by US air power, and Castro's troops proved stronger than the invasion force.[7] More than 100 invaders died and around 1,200 were captured (five were subsequently executed for leading the invasion).[8] Most significantly, the Cuban people stood solidly behind Castro.

A disastrous result

President Kennedy's first major foreign policy effort had gone catastrophically wrong. Some people thought the United States should have given more support to the invasion. Others blamed the CIA for giving the president inaccurate information. It had

Captured Cuban exiles in April 1961, guarded by Castro's soldiers. The exiles were part of the group that attempted to invade Cuba at the Bay of Pigs.

Operation Mongoose

After the Bay of Pigs fiasco, President Kennedy looked for alternative ways to remove Castro. In November 1961, he established Operation Mongoose, a secret plan aimed at bringing down the Castro regime. Bobby Kennedy was in charge. At a White House meeting, Bobby scribbled these notes:

> "My idea is to stir things up on the island with espionage [spying], **sabotage**, general disorder, run and operated by Cubans themselves with every group but Batistaites [supporters of Batista] and Communists. Do not know if we will be successful in overthrowing Castro but we have nothing to lose in my estimate."[10]

Operation Mongoose also spread anti-Castro political propaganda (information meant to promote a point of view) and supported **guerrilla** raids by anti-Castro activists. A variety of CIA plots to assassinate Castro were later uncovered, although no written order from Bobby or John Kennedy to carry out such an action was ever found. Another aspect to the operation was economic—trying to prevent countries from trading with Cuba, in order to put pressure on the regime.[11] Years after Operation Mongoose officially ended, other U.S. government agencies continued to carry out sabotage against Cuba.[12]

To read more about Operation Mongoose, go to www.pbs.org/wgbh/amex/rfk/peopleevents/e_mongoose.html.

misjudged Castro's strength, while overestimating the likelihood that the Cuban people would support the exiles. Kennedy learned his lesson: he resolved never to rely on the opinions of the generals again.[9] Although the Cuban exiles pressed for further action against Castro, Kennedy would think extremely carefully about launching another direct attack on Cuban soil.

What do you think?:

Was the United States right to try to bring down Castro?

Starting in February 1961, Castro sent Cuban agents to encourage revolution in other Latin American countries, such as Nicaragua, Venezuela, and Argentina.[13] In 1966, guerrilla leader Che Guevara went to Bolivia to establish an anti-government force there. Given that Castro was trying to promote other revolutions, was the United States justified in trying to stop him?

Battle over Berlin

The thorny issue of Berlin presented another Cold War dilemma. After World War II, the German city of Berlin was divided into four sectors. The Soviet Union controlled East Berlin, while the United States, Great Britain, and France governed the three sectors of West Berlin.

This map shows the division of Berlin after World War II. A large part of the city was controlled by Western powers, although Berlin was in East Germany.

In 1958, Soviet leader Nikita Khrushchev demanded that all troops move from West Berlin and leave it under Soviet control. He aimed to take control of the entire city to stop people from migrating from Soviet-ruled East Berlin to the West.

The United States and other Western powers could not accept this demand. East Germans continued to leave in the tens of thousands.[14] At the Vienna **summit** of 1961, Khrushchev restated his position, but President Kennedy maintained that the West should retain access to Berlin. Kennedy anticipated a confrontation in Berlin. Since both sides possessed nuclear weapons, it could potentially lead to nuclear war.

Talk or fight?

Should President Kennedy pursue negotiations or military action? Kennedy asked special advisor Dean Acheson, who was involved with foreign affairs, to look at the options. In mid-June 1961, Acheson suggested moving troops to Europe, in an effort to show Khrushchev that the United States would challenge his attempt to take over West Berlin.

However, another adviser, Arthur Schlesinger, opposed this position. He believed the Soviet Union wanted to avoid clashing with the West over Berlin and would be prepared to negotiate. Along with others, Schlesinger wrote to the president calling for a flexible response: the United States should offer negotiations, while also undertaking military preparations.[15]

President Kennedy chose the second option: building up military forces in Europe, while continuing with diplomatic efforts to avoid the risk of nuclear war.[16] He felt that the stronger the West's military position, the better bargain he could make.[17]

In August, Khrushchev adopted a different solution to the problem of citizens leaving East Berlin. He constructed the Berlin Wall, a 15-foot- (5-metre-) high barrier to divide the East from the West. Kennedy's combination of military preparedness and negotiation had caused his opponent to retreat. The Berlin Wall became a symbol of opposition to communism—a successful outcome for Kennedy.[18]

Decisive words: Kennedy defends West Berlin

On July 25, 1961, President Kennedy made a speech blaming the Berlin crisis on the Soviet Union. He set out his twin policies of **diplomacy** backed by the willingness to use force, saying:

"So long as the Communists insist that they are preparing to end by themselves unilaterally [alone] our rights in West Berlin and our commitments to its people, we must be prepared to defend those rights and those commitments. We will at all times be ready to talk, if talk will help. But we must also be ready to resist with force, if force is used upon us. Either alone would fail. Together, they can serve the cause of freedom and peace."[19]

Laos

When Kennedy's presidency began, **civil war** raged in Laos, in Southeast Asia. Why did this concern the United States?

Like Berlin, Laos was caught up in the Cold War. China had turned communist in 1949, and North Vietnam had followed in 1954. Since 1959, Laos had endured a civil war fought among communists under Pathet Lao, pro-Western forces, and neutral forces (those not aligned to the West or to communism). The United States hoped to halt the tide of communism that was sweeping across Southeast Asia.[20]

In December 1960, right-wing (conservative) general Phoumi Nosavan, assisted by the CIA, had taken control of the government of Laos. The ousted neutralist leader, Souvanna Phouma, joined with Pathet Lao's communists to fight Phoumi.

President Eisenhower, the outgoing US president, recommended that President Kennedy continue to support Phoumi.[21] But Kennedy was uncertain. Communist forces in Laos were strong, while anti-communist forces were weak. At the start of 1961, Pathet Lao gained more territory. Kennedy had to craft a strategy. Concerned about a communist victory in Laos, he also wanted to avoid being dragged into an unwinnable war.

According to a Special National Intelligence Estimate of February 1961, Phoumi's army could defeat Pathet Lao. So, Kennedy chose to back Phoumi, as a counterbalance to the communists.

However, the communists led a stronger fight back, and by March, Phoumi was in retreat.[22] The United States was backing a loser. The US decided to bring in more military

The case against the invasion of Laos

The U.S. government realized it was too hazardous to invade Laos, for a variety of reasons:

- Local communist troops knew the terrain (land); U.S. troops would not.

- The United States could introduce Thai troops into Laos, but the communists could retaliate by bringing in soldiers from North Vietnam.

- The United States could use fighter aircraft to disrupt supply lines, but Soviet or Chinese aircraft could counter this.

- Intervention in Laos risked provoking a larger-scale war in Southeast Asia.[26]

advisers and then additional forces. It hoped that the threat of significant US military involvement would persuade the communists to back down.[23]

However, it became clear that Pathet Lao had no intention to surrender. In March, Senator Mike Mansfield advised the president that prolonged military involvement would probably make the situation in Laos worse, leading to a larger-scale war.[24] In April, the Bay of Pigs invasion took place. Afterward, Kennedy returned to the Laos problem. The fiasco in Cuba influenced his decision.

Learning from experience

The failure of the Bay of Pigs invasion made President Kennedy cautious when considering whether to launch military intervention in Laos. He said: "Thank God the Bay of Pigs happened when it did. Otherwise we'd be in Laos by now—and that would be a hundred times worse."[27]

The neutral option

President Kennedy believed the risks of intervention were too high because of the great weakness of anti-communist forces, so he resolved to back a neutralist solution. In May 1961, there was a cease-fire in Laos. In the fall, the parties agreed to form a neutral coalition government made up of the communists, the right wing, and neutral forces.[25] But the coalition fell apart in 1964, and Laos subsequently became engulfed in the Vietnam conflict.

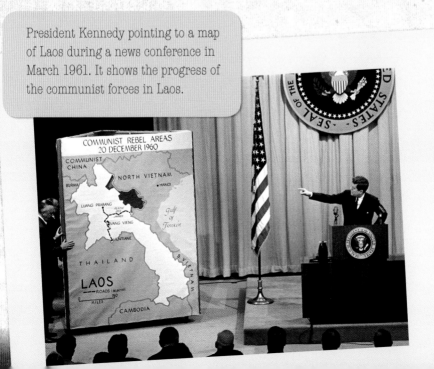

President Kennedy pointing to a map of Laos during a news conference in March 1961. It shows the progress of the communist forces in Laos.

The Cuban Missile Crisis Develops

Since the 1950s, as part of the Cold War (see page 9), U.S. and Soviet military strategy had focused on building nuclear weapons that could be used against each other in a conflict. In 1962, Khrushchev decided to base nuclear missiles in Cuba, close to the United States. It led to a furious reaction from the United States and brought the world close to nuclear war.

Khrushchev did not plan to use the missiles on Cuba.[1] So, why did he position them there? There were several reasons:

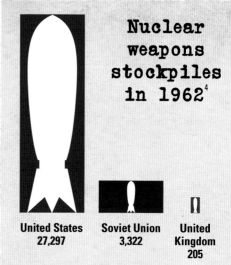

Nuclear weapons stockpiles in 1962[4]

United States	Soviet Union	United Kingdom
27,297	3,322	205

- He hoped to protect Cuba after the Bay of Pigs invasion (see pages 16 and 17) and believed it was acceptable to support an ally in this way.[2]

- Khrushchev wanted to reinforce the Soviet military position. The United States had just placed missiles in Turkey, close to the Soviet border, that could wipe out Soviet cities. Placing missiles in Cuba, close to the United States, was a way of evening up the score—as Khrushchev said, "to scare them, to restrain them...to give them back some of their own medicine."[3]

- Cuba wanted protection—but the Soviet Union used this as a pretext (false reason) for its own goal to install nuclear missiles.

Was the Soviet Union naïve?

Khrushchev believed that the arrival of nuclear weapons could take place secretly. He assumed the United States would think that the Soviet Union was providing **conventional** (non-nuclear) defense forces for Cuba. Somehow, he believed that U.S. spy planes would not spot the nuclear materials arriving on the island, right on their doorstep.

Kennedy's reaction

President Kennedy had a different perspective. The United States had promised to protect West Berlin from takeover by the Soviet Union (see pages 18 and 19). But West Berlin was surrounded by Soviet troops. The only way the United States could defend it was by threatening to use nuclear weapons against the Soviets. If President Kennedy did not strongly demand that Khrushchev remove his missiles from Cuba, Khrushchev might think Kennedy would not be tough when it came to the US pledge to defend Berlin.[5]

The contrasting perspectives of the Soviet Union and the United States led to the Cuban Missile Crisis–with the small country of Cuba stuck in the middle and likely to suffer the worst consequences of conflict. So, how did the crisis unfold?

The famous aerial photograph taken by a U.S. spy plane showing a missile launch site in San Cristóbal, Cuba. This alerted the United States to the Soviet delivery of nuclear weapons to Cuba.

What do you think?:

Should—and could—Castro have rejected nuclear missiles?

Castro was pleased to have a defense system to protect Cuba against another invasion. But a conventional force would have been adequate. It was the placing of nuclear missiles that caused a crisis in international relations. Castro agreed to accept the missiles, but he was not happy about it.[6] Could Castro have persuaded the Soviet Union to provide a non-nuclear defense force in Cuba?

Panic in the United States

On August 29, 1962, special cameras in U.S. spy planes flying over Cuba photographed military buildings and Soviet technicians. When the U.S. government challenged Khrushchev, he initially denied that he was constructing missile bases, and then he claimed they were purely defensive.

President Kennedy's government did not trust this assertion. Kennedy asked Secretary of Defense Robert McNamara to initiate secret plans for military operations against Cuba, in case they proved necessary. A week later, on September 7, Kennedy asked Congress for approval to call up 150,000 reservists.[7] He announced that a military exercise would take place in the Caribbean in October. Kennedy also asked his brother Bobby to step up the activities of Operation Mongoose, aimed at toppling Castro (see page 17).

On October 14, the United States found evidence of Soviet offensive weapons in Cuba. A spy plane took photos of a **ballistic missile** on a launching site. Two days later, McGeorge Bundy, Kennedy's

Nikita Sergeyevich Khrushchev 1894–1971

Born: Kalinovka, Russia

Role: Leader of the Soviet Union, 1958–1964

Upon becoming leader of the Soviet Union, Nikita Sergeyevich Khrushchev stated his policy of coexisting peacefully with the non-communist world. He visited the United States in 1959, and relations between the two countries improved for a short time. However, at the Vienna summit in 1961 (see page 18), no agreement was reached over Berlin, and Khrushchev then built the Berlin Wall (see page 19). Khrushchev also reduced conventional weapons and developed more nuclear missiles to counter the United States' larger nuclear force. He tried to secretly locate medium-range missiles in Cuba in 1962, resulting in an international crisis. After the Cuban Missile Crisis was resolved, he signed the Limited Test Ban Treaty with the United States in 1963 (see page 42). Khrushchev's handling of the Cuban Missile Crisis was a major factor in his downfall in 1964, when his deputy, Leonid Brezhnev, seized power.

Did you know? After his fall from grace, Khrushchev secretly dictated his memoirs (life story). They were published in the United States and Europe in 1970—but not in the Soviet Union.[9]

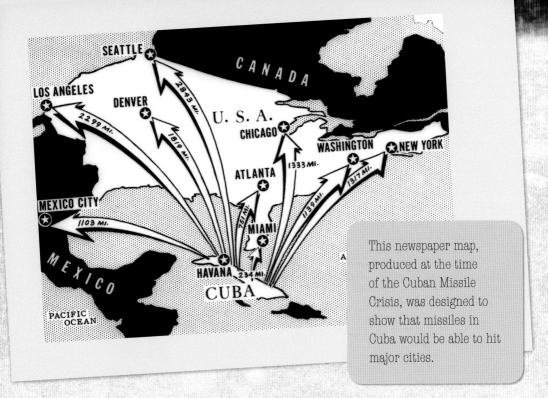

SEATTLE
LOS ANGELES
DENVER
CANADA
U.S.A.
CHICAGO
WASHINGTON
NEW YORK
ATLANTA
2843 MI.
2299 MI.
1819 MI.
1333 MI.
1317 MI.
1139 MI.
MEXICO CITY
1103 MI.
757 MI.
MIAMI
HAVANA
234 MI.
CUBA
MEXICO
PACIFIC OCEAN

This newspaper map, produced at the time of the Cuban Missile Crisis, was designed to show that missiles in Cuba would be able to hit major cities.

special assistant for national security affairs, broke the news to the president. The CIA reported that once installed, the missiles on Cuba would have the power to kill more than 80 million Americans in a matter of minutes.[8] Their installation was a massive provocation to the United States.

President Kennedy rapidly formed an advisory team, the Executive Committee of the National Security Council (also known as ExComm), to plan a response. It included Secretary of State Dean Rusk, Secretary of Defense Robert McNamara, Chairman of the Joint Chiefs of Staff General Maxwell Taylor, and Bobby Kennedy.

In the United States and across the world, people were genuinely terrified that a nuclear war was about to erupt.

Eliminate Cuba?

The U.S. government may have considered a nuclear strike on Cuba. On October 16, U.S. Secretary of State Dean Rusk stated at a meeting at the White House: "I think we have to think very hard about two major courses of action as alternatives. One is the quick strike... I don't think this in itself would require an invasion of Cuba... Or we're going to decide that this is the time to eliminate [get rid of] the Cuba problem by actually eliminating the island."[10]

Discussing the options

During the tense days of the Cuban Missile Crisis, members of Kennedy's ExComm held many strategy meetings. At first, the argument for military action appeared strongest. The Joint Chiefs of Staff favored a full invasion of Cuba. They did not believe the Soviet Union would react to a takeover of Cuba. But Kennedy resisted this option because the results could not be predicted, saying, "Nobody knows what kind of success we're going to have with this invasion. Invasions are tough, hazardous."[11] He wanted to discuss all the possibilities before taking action.

Kennedy's options during the Cuban Missile Crisis

The following chart shows the options President Kennedy was faced with in the Cuban Missile Crisis, as well as their likely consequences:

Option	Likely consequence
Ignore the missiles	Very bad politically. The Soviet Union could take advantage.
Request that the Soviet Union remove the missiles	Unlikely to work
Negotiate with the Soviet Union, offering to withdraw US missiles in Turkey and Italy in return for the removal of Soviet missiles in Cuba	Could possibly work, but might not be effective without a show of force
Naval blockade around Cuba to prevent ships with offensive weapons from entering or leaving	Would buy time while planning negotiations or military action
Air strike against the missile bases	Would cause casualties (death and injury) among Soviets and could kill Cuban civilians (people not involved in the armed services). This would make the problem become even more intense.
Military invasion of Cuba	Could cause heavy American as well as Soviet and Cuban casualties
Launch nuclear weapons against Cuba and/or the Soviet Union	Would have led to the Soviet forces firing nuclear missiles in return, causing massive casualties and possibly leading to worldwide nuclear war[12]

President Kennedy holding one of the tense daily ExComm meetings during the crisis of October 1962.

A quarantine

Robert McNamara suggested a naval **blockade** around Cuba. After heated discussions, on October 20, President Kennedy resolved to adopt this policy if the Soviet Union refused to withdraw the missiles immediately. Kennedy called the blockade a "**quarantine**," because "blockade" is a wartime term and he wanted to stress that the United States was not at war. The quarantine would buy time for negotiations. However, Kennedy did not rule out the use of military force. As in Berlin and Laos, he knew that possessing military might was a powerful tool in negotiations. If Khrushchev failed to cave in, a US air attack and invasion of Cuba would follow.

Robert McNamara 1919–2009

Born: San Francisco, California

Role: U.S. Secretary of Defense, 1961–1968

Robert McNamara was President Kennedy's secretary of defense. Following Kennedy's guidance, he rejected the strategy of a first strike on an enemy. Instead, he focused on building sufficient **arms** to deter a nuclear strike and to counterattack if necessary—but avoiding massive retaliation.[13] During the Cuban Missile Crisis, McNamara was one of Kennedy's most trusted advisers and played a key role in decision-making. At first, McNamara favored an air attack on Cuba, but he switched to supporting the quarantine policy. McNamara helped Kennedy to control the military leaders and prevent them from embarking on armed action against Cuba.[14]

Did you know? Before he entered government, McNamara was president of the Ford Motor Company.

The speech

After a week of crisis meetings, on October 22, President Kennedy broadcast a speech on television to inform the American people of the situation. He explained that the Soviet Union was building nuclear missile bases in Cuba with weapons capable of striking the United States.[15] He demanded that Khrushchev remove the missiles. Kennedy's speech was designed to unite Americans and to put pressure on Khrushchev. Kennedy also wrote to Khrushchev, appealing to him to withdraw the weapons.

Decisive words: A warning

In Kennedy's speech on October 22, he put the blame squarely on the Soviet Union for the crisis, saying that the "deception" of trying to place missiles on Cuba secretly, and the "sudden change in…deployment [placing]" of these lethal weapons presented a serious danger to the world. He went on to say:

"Neither the United States of America nor the world community of nations can tolerate deliberate deception and offensive threats on the part of any nation, large or small. We no longer live in a world where only the actual firing of weapons represents an efficient challenge to a nation's security to constitute maximum peril [serious danger]. Nuclear weapons are so destructive and ballistic missiles are so swift, that any substantially increased possibility of their use or any sudden change in their deployment may well be regarded as a definite threat to peace."[16]

A Cuban refugee living in Miami watches Kennedy's television address on October 22. Many Cuban refugees hoped that Kennedy would take action against Fidel Castro.

U.S. forces ready for action

President Kennedy backed up his strong words with a demonstration of might. On October 22, the British *Daily Mail* newspaper reported: "A massive buildup of American forces in the Caribbean this weekend started rumors throughout the United States of an impending invasion of Cuba."[17]

The following day, Khrushchev wrote to Kennedy, claiming that the missiles were for defense purposes only. Kennedy did not accept Khrushchev's explanation and ordered the quarantine to begin the next day. He announced, "All ships of any kind bound for Cuba from whatever nation or port will, if found to contain cargoes of offensive weapons, be turned back."[18]

October 27: In the UK, anti-nuclear protesters demonstrate against the United States' handling of the crisis, arguing against a war over Cuba.

Western governments, including those of West Germany, Great Britain, France, and Canada, backed Kennedy. The Organization of American States (an organization for regional cooperation, which had suspended Cuba in January 1962) also lent its support. British Prime Minister Harold Macmillan agreed to back the United States, although he was unsure if the blockade was legal.[19] However, some people in Britain held protests against the possession of nuclear weapons.[20]

The Soviet Union and China supported Cuba. Fearing an impending invasion, Castro placed his armed forces on alert and mobilized 270,000 reservists.

Blockade!

On October 24, the United States began its blockade of Cuban waters, in the hope of forcing Khrushchev to withdraw the missiles from Cuba. The U.S. government could not predict if this move would prevent war.

During the October blockade, a U.S. Navy ship intercepts a Soviet ship leaving Cuba carrying missiles. Most Soviet ship captains cooperated readily with the blockade although a few had to be persuaded to show their cargo.

The U.S. Navy deployed its ships to stop and search vessels going to Cuba, to prevent them from bringing arms. Other goods, such as food, could be delivered. At this time, U.S. intelligence was reporting that the Soviet technicians had nearly completed their missile sites on Cuba. It was likely that some Soviet ships heading to Cuba would contain weapons.

The United States could not be sure that the Soviet craft would observe its quarantine. In the morning, ExComm heard that two Soviet ships, apparently carrying "offensive weapons," were heading toward the quarantine line. What would happen if a vessel resisted a U.S. Navy search? President Kennedy wanted to avoid a confrontation that could lead to Soviet deaths and increase the tension further.[1] Later that morning, a report came through to ExComm that all six Soviet ships in Cuban waters had turned back. Relieved, Rusk commented to Bundy: "We're eyeball to eyeball, and I think the other fellow just blinked."[2]

An appeal from the United Nations

The United Nations (UN) became involved to try to prevent disaster. Also on October 24, U Thant, the acting secretary-general of the UN, appealed to Khrushchev to suspend arms shipments to Cuba and requested that Kennedy stop the blockade for a few weeks while the issue was sorted out.[3] Would the world leaders agree to break the **impasse**?

Publicly, Khrushchev would not budge. That evening, he sent a harsh letter stating that he would not respect the blockade and would protect Soviet rights. Yet behind the scenes, he held a private meeting with a trusted U.S. businessman in Moscow and said that, in fact, he was prepared to talk. He expected the message to be passed on to the U.S. government.[4] Kennedy responded to Khrushchev's public message and stressed that he would not give in. A glimmer of hope for resolution had appeared, but the situation remained grave.

The Cuban reaction

Most Cubans accepted the missiles and supported their government. Life went on as normal. U.S. historian Robert Quirk wrote in his biography of Castro: "The overwhelming majority in October 1962 stood by their government in the crisis, as they had done at the time of the Bay of Pigs invasion, some because they supported the social and economic reforms, others because for them a sense of national pride came before economic well-being."[5]

Decisive words: Castro threatens the United States

Castro responded angrily to the quarantine policy. In a speech on October 23, he claimed that Kennedy was trying to prevent Cuba from protecting itself, called Kennedy a "pirate" for introducing the quarantine, and said the United States was acting as an agent of "fascism," linking the U.S. government to the Nazis who had murdered millions during World War II. He then issued a powerful nuclear threat against the United States, saying:

"The people should know the following: we have the means with which to repel a direct attack… We are running risks that we have no choice but to run… We have the consolation of knowing that in a thermo-nuclear war, the aggressors, those who unleash a thermo-nuclear war, will be exterminated [killed]."[6]

Khrushchev makes a move

Next, Khrushchev publicly took the initiative, replying to a letter from well-known philosopher and anti-nuclear campaigner Bertrand Russell to say he would "take no reckless decisions" and suggesting a summit.[7] He recommended a U.S. pledge not to invade Cuba in return for the dismantling of the Soviet missiles, saying, "As long as rocket-nuclear weapons have not been used there is a possibility of averting war. Once the Americans have launched aggression, a summit meeting will become impossible and useless."[8]

This was a positive development. Why did Khrushchev make the first move? In the face of massive U.S. power, it was clear he could not win a conflict in the region. Yet he could use the opportunity to portray himself as a man of peace.[9]

On October 25, both Kennedy and Khrushchev responded to U Thant's plea for calm, agreeing that they desired a peaceful

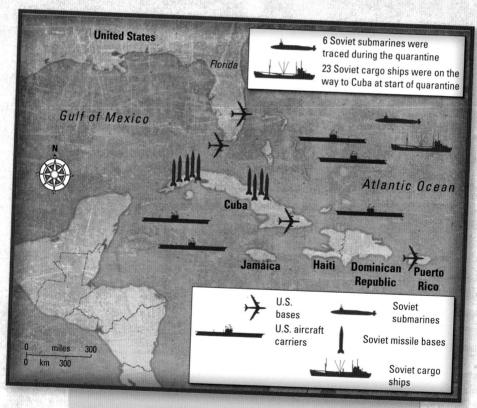

United States

Florida

6 Soviet submarines were traced during the quarantine

23 Soviet cargo ships were on the way to Cuba at start of quarantine

Gulf of Mexico

N

Atlantic Ocean

Cuba

Jamaica   Haiti   Dominican   Puerto
                    Republic   Rico

| 0 | miles | 300 |
| 0 | km | 300 |

U.S. bases

U.S. aircraft carriers

Soviet submarines

Soviet missile bases

Soviet cargo ships

This map shows the balance of forces in the Caribbean during the Cuban Missile Crisis. The United States had its forces on alert at several military bases in the region.

Confrontation at the UN

Even though the leaders of the United States and Soviet Union had told U Thant they desired a peaceful resolution, a confrontation erupted between the U.S. ambassador and the Soviet ambassador at a UN meeting on October 25. The U.S. ambassador to the UN claimed that the Soviet Union had failed to admit that it had installed medium- and intermediate-range ballistic missiles in Cuba that could hit the United States. He held up the photos taken by the U.S. spy plane on October 14 and challenged the Soviet ambassador to reply. The Soviet ambassador declined to comment.[12]

solution. Khrushchev offered to suspend arms shipments to Cuba for a short time if Kennedy avoided confronting Soviet ships.[10] However, he did not agree to stop building missile bases in Cuba.

Meanwhile, it appeared that Kennedy's gamble over the quarantine policy had paid off. On October 25, the U.S. Navy intercepted the first Soviet ship. After an inspection, it was allowed to proceed without incident. The following day, a Lebanese ship chartered by the Soviet Union was also stopped, inspected, and permitted to continue.[11] If a U.S. patrol had tried to carry out a search and had been refused, the crisis could have rapidly deepened.

The army wants action

At the ExComm meeting on October 26, discussions focused on what should be done next. The quarantine had been respected and was no longer the main issue. What should the United States do about the missiles that Khrushchev was unwilling to withdraw? Should they launch a bombing attack or negotiate? The Joint Chiefs of Staff demanded military action. Once again, Kennedy held his nerve.

Robert Kennedy urges caution

Bobby Kennedy had a strong influence on his brother John, and he opposed an air strike against Cuba from the beginning. He believed there would be wider consequences if the United States initiated military action. On October 16, he had stated:

"You're going to kill an awful lot of people [with an air strike] and we are going to take a lot of heat for it... You're going to announce the reason that you're doing it is because they're sending this kind of missiles, well, I think it's almost incumbent upon the Russians [they are obliged] then to say, 'Well, we're going to send them in again, and if you do it again...we're going to do the same thing to Turkey or...Iran.'"[13]

33

Negotiate or bomb?

On October 26, Bobby Kennedy held an unofficial meeting with the Soviet ambassador Anatoly Dobrynin. Dobrynin stated that if the United States found Soviet missiles located in Cuba to be unacceptable, then U.S. missiles located in Turkey were also unacceptable, for the same reasons. He was implying that if the Soviet Union were to back down over Cuba, it would require an action from the United States in return. Removing U.S. missiles from Turkey would be the perfect response, and it would allow Khrushchev to save face.

Robert F. Kennedy 1925–1968

Born: Brookline, Massachusetts

Role: U.S. attorney general (head of the Department of Justice) and adviser to John F. Kennedy

John F. Kennedy's brother Robert F. Kennedy—known as Bobby—was his closest adviser. During the Cuban Missile Crisis, Bobby often chaired the meetings of ExComm and led unofficial "**back channel**" discussions with the Soviet ambassador Anatoly Dobrynin. After John Kennedy's death, Bobby Kennedy followed in his brother's footsteps. He became a U.S. senator in 1965 and campaigned for the presidential nomination. However, in 1968 he, too, was assassinated.[15]

Did you know?
Unusually for a white politician at the time, Bobby Kennedy argued that African Americans should be included in professional sports.

Bobby Kennedy called the president to check what he thought. Dobrynin sent Bobby's reply to the Soviet Foreign Ministry on October 27, explaining that if the U.S. missiles in Turkey were the only issue preventing an end to the crisis, then the United States could find a way to remove them.[14]

On October 26, Khrushchev wrote to Kennedy proposing a deal. He offered to remove the Soviet missiles if the United States agreed not to invade Cuba. The following day, Khrushchev sent a second letter with conditions: if the Soviet Union were to withdraw missiles from Cuba, then the United States should also remove missiles from Turkey. It appeared the message from Dobrynin had now reached Khrushchev, and he realized he could make a better bargain with the United States.

In the United States, the issue was becoming increasingly urgent. The CIA was monitoring the preparation of the missile launchers in Cuba. Day by day, more missiles were becoming operational. If a deal was going to be struck, there was no time to lose.

Decisive words: Khrushchev's offer

The following is a crucial part of Khrushchev's first letter on October 26, in which he clarified the deal he was prepared to make with the United States, saying:

"We, for our part, will declare that our ships, bound for Cuba, will not carry any kind of armaments [weapons]. You would declare that the United States will not invade Cuba with its forces and will not support any sort of forces which might intend to carry out an invasion of Cuba. Then the necessity for the presence of our military specialists in Cuba would disappear."[16]

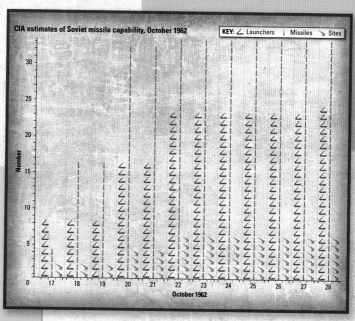

This chart shows the United States' intelligence estimates of the rapidly growing capability of the Soviet forces in Cuba during October 1962. Day by day, more missiles were becoming operational.

Resolution and Aftermath

On October 27, the United States and Soviet Union were on the brink of war. President Kennedy's decisions at this crucial time would affect world history.

On that day, ExComm discussed Khrushchev's proposals for four hours. The group agreed that withdrawing the missiles from Turkey would weaken the North Atlantic Treaty Organization (NATO) military alliance and make it look as though the United States was backing down. Kennedy was unsure; he thought that perhaps the missiles should be discussed.

But news had just come through to ExComm that a U.S. U-2 spy plane had been shot down over Cuba, and its pilot had been killed. Incensed, the Joint Chiefs of Staff pushed for an air strike, to be followed by an invasion in a week.[1]

Mobilizing for war...

President Kennedy was unwilling to act immediately. However, like the army chiefs, Kennedy was aware that the missile sites on Cuba were nearly ready for action. He ordered the mobilization of more U.S. forces and made plans for an invasion. Kennedy ordered the State Department to make preparations for establishing a new government in Cuba afterward.

Close to nuclear war

In 2002, on the 40th anniversary of the Cuban Missile Crisis, academics and officials from Cuba, the United States, and the former Soviet Union held a conference to discuss documents that had formerly been secret. They discovered that the world had been closer to nuclear war than anyone realized at the time. On October 27, 1962, a Soviet submarine had been depth-charged (bombed) by a U.S. destroyer carrying a nuclear weapon. The captain of the Soviet submarine had told the crew to load a nuclear-tipped torpedo but then, fortunately for the whole world, he decided to surface instead of firing it.[2]

To find out about the 40th anniversary conference, go to: www.gwu.edu/%7Ensarchiv/nsa/cuba_mis_cri.

As part of the preparations for a possible invasion of Cuba, U.S. soldiers practice a beach landing during training at Fort Pierce in Florida.

...yet aiming for peace

As a possible way out of the impasse, some advisers recommended replying positively to Khrushchev's first letter and ignoring the second one (see page 35).[3] Bobby Kennedy advised his brother not to pass up the opportunity for a resolution of the crisis. This could be the last chance to avoid military conflict. Knowing that if he made the wrong decision, millions could die, President Kennedy opted for negotiation.

President Kennedy wrote to Khrushchev, accepting the terms in his October 26 letter, but ignoring the request to remove missiles from Turkey in the October 27 letter. If the Soviet Union removed the missiles, the United States would end the quarantine and promise not to invade Cuba.

But Kennedy gave his opponent an ultimatum (final statement of terms): if the Soviet Union failed to respond by October 29, the United States would launch an invasion. As Bobby Kennedy told Dobrynin directly: "If they did not remove those bases then we would remove them."[4] The Soviet response over the next 24 hours would determine the result: war or peace.

What do you think?:

Who was the peacemaker?

Should Khrushchev be given the credit for offering negotiations in his letter to Kennedy of October 26? Or does Kennedy deserve more credit because he fended off the army chiefs' desire for immediate military action and responded to Khrushchev's offer?

The secret deal

To the world, it appeared as though the United States was on the verge of invading Cuba. But as soon as President Kennedy had sent his response to Khrushchev, Bobby Kennedy contacted Dobrynin through the unofficial "back channel" and made a secret offer. If Khrushchev accepted Kennedy's public promise not to attack Cuba, U.S. missiles in Turkey would quietly be removed once the Cuban crisis was resolved.[5] Thus, he secretly agreed to Khrushchev's demand in his second letter on October 27. The public was completely unaware of these discussions.

At this point, without bothering to consult Castro, Khrushchev opted for retreat. In a broadcast, he announced that the missiles in Cuba would be dismantled and removed. At the same time, he sent a secret message to Kennedy saying he was pleased that Kennedy had promised to remove weapons from Turkey in four or five months and that he would not reveal this private pact.[6] For his part, Kennedy agreed not to invade the island. On October 29, an agreement was made.

The world had stepped back from the brink of war. On November 20, Kennedy formally announced that the crisis was over. Yet he noted: "We will not, of course, abandon the political, economic, and other efforts of this hemisphere to halt **subversion** from Cuba, nor our purpose and hope that the Cuban people shall some day be wholly free."[7] It was clear that the United States would not tolerate communism near its shores.

Timeline: October 1962

This timeline shows crucial events in October 1962:

October 14
The United States discovers evidence of Soviet offensive weapons in Cuba.

October 16
President Kennedy is informed about the Soviet missile sites in Cuba. He sets up ExComm.

October 29
An agreement is reached.

October 28
Khrushchev announces that the Soviet Union will remove the missiles and accepts a secret deal under which the United States would remove the missiles from Turkey.

Khrushchev making a speech at the time of the Cuban Missile Crisis. In late October, he realized that events were spiraling out of control and decided to back down.

Positive reactions: The communist world

In the communist world, Khrushchev claimed a victory for the Soviet Union, saying: "We had been able to extract from Kennedy a promise that neither America nor her allies would invade Cuba."[8] Although the Soviet media was tightly controlled, it appeared that ordinary people were pleased that the threat of war had lifted. The same seemed to be true in Cuba.

Congratulations to Khrushchev

Communist parties around the world supported the Soviet Union. They gave credit to Khrushchev for ending the crisis and did not admit that he had backed down. The following extract appeared in the *Daily Worker*, the newspaper of the British Communist Party, on October 29:

"The whole world welcomes Mr. Khruschev's efforts to pull mankind back from the abyss of the nuclear war... His willingness to withdraw the weapons... proves that these weapons were there to defend Cuba."[9]

October 20
Kennedy decides on a naval quarantine around Cuba.

October 22
Kennedy mobilizes U.S. forces around Cuba.

October 24
The quarantine begins. Soviet ships turn back from Cuba.

October 27
Khrushchev sends a second letter demanding that the United States also remove its missiles from Turkey. Kennedy responds to the first letter and threatens military action if the Soviet Union does not respond by October 29.

October 26
Khrushchev writes to Kennedy, offering to remove the missiles if Kennedy does not invade Cuba.

Congratulations in the West

From the perspective of the United States, the Soviet Union had surrendered to U.S. demands, so the crisis resulted in a victory for the West. Many Americans glossed over the fact that Khrushchev had made the proposal that ended the crisis. In the United States and other Western countries, praise was heaped on President Kennedy and his advisers for avoiding war and adopting a wise political strategy that did not humiliate their opponent.[10] But Kennedy specifically told the ExComm members: "Don't gloat, don't boast, don't take any pride in victory."[11] Kennedy's success was reflected in the November elections for Congress, when the Democrats increased their majority.

What do you think?:

Was Kennedy responsible for the peaceful settlement?

Kennedy did not believe it was his own great skill that had achieved a peaceful settlement, but he acknowledged other reasons for success. Perhaps it was due to the United States' military superiority in the region, as the U.S. Navy had deployed its power in a massive show of force. Admiral Robert Lee Dennison, unified commander for the Caribbean, readied army, air force, marine, and naval forces for a possible invasion of Cuba, although, ultimately, it was not necessary to resort to war.[15] Also, Moscow did not have a great need for missiles on Cuba and could not have justified launching a nuclear conflict over this small island. Nevertheless, Kennedy played a significant role in resisting pressure for air attacks and invasion.[16] Was Kennedy being modest, or did the strength of the U.S. military forces ensure a successful outcome?

Negative reactions

But not everyone celebrated the outcome. General Curtis Le May, for example, thought Kennedy had acted with weakness and should have attacked Cuba. Many Cuban exiles felt betrayed, because they had hoped the United States would topple Fidel Castro.

Within Cuba itself, Castro was furious. He felt that his country had been treated like a pawn in the superpowers' game. Castro had not asked for missiles in the first place, and no one had consulted him about withdrawing them. On October 28, he issued a statement offering his point of view. It listed five demands, which he believed should have been included in the bargain Khrushchev

Military madness?

President Kennedy stood by his decision, and he was highly critical of his military leaders. He told his aide Schlesinger: "An invasion would have been a mistake—a wrong use of our power. But the military are mad. They wanted to do this."[17]

A group of Cuban exiles jeering at police during a protest in Washington, D.C. in 1964. They were demanding U.S. military action to topple Castro.

made with Kennedy. They included an end to the United States' refusal to trade with Cuba and to its acts of subversion against his government.[12]

The official Cuban historian of the Cuban Missile Crisis, Tomás Diez Acosta, also criticized the Soviet Union for failing to consider Cuban interests, saying: "In any proposed exchange, it would have been more honorable for the Soviets—and a matter of elementary justice for the Cubans—to have demanded first of all the return of territory illegally occupied by the Guantánamo naval base and the withdrawal of U.S. troops stationed there."[13] The United States had controlled the naval base since 1903, and Cuba had always protested its presence.[14] But the U.S.–Soviet agreement brought no benefits for Cuba.

The aftermath of crisis

In accordance with the agreement, the Soviet Union removed its weapons from Cuba. In 1963, the United States withdrew its missiles from Turkey, as secretly agreed. To speed up communications between American and Soviet leaders in any future crisis, a "hotline," meaning a direct phone line, was installed between Washington, D.C., and Moscow.

The Limited Test Ban Treaty

In late 1962, President Kennedy began negotiating with the other nations that had nuclear weapons—the Soviet Union and Great Britain—to ban the testing of nuclear weapons. He believed this would help to stop the escalating arms race. A ban might inhibit nuclear powers from making bombs and therefore reduce the risk of nuclear war. It could reduce the likelihood of other countries deciding to develop them. Additionally, it could improve relations with the Soviet Union.

On August 5, 1963, the United States, Soviet Union, and Great Britain signed the Limited Test Ban Treaty, agreeing in principle to ban the testing of nuclear weapons. Some historians contend that this was Kennedy's greatest foreign policy success. It was the first arms control agreement and an important step toward reducing the tensions between the Soviet Union and the West,

President Kennedy, in the company of a group of senators, signs the Limited Test Ban Treaty. According to the treaty, all tests of nuclear weapons were banned, except for those conducted underground.

prompting hope for an end to the Cold War.[18] However, the Cold War continued for nearly three more decades, and several more countries developed nuclear weapons.

The improvement of relations was a key concern for Kennedy. In his "peace speech" of June 10, 1963, he argued for a more sympathetic attitude toward the Soviet Union. The speech received little attention in the United States at the time, but it was well received in the Soviet Union.[19] Although the Cold War did continue, there was never any direct military conflict between the United States and Soviet Union.

Decisive words: Kennedy's "peace speech"

In President Kennedy's speech at American University on June 10, 1963, he dismissed the idea that the world could survive a nuclear war, saying:

"I speak of peace because of the new face of war. Total war makes no sense in an age when great powers can maintain large and relatively invulnerable [impossible to defeat] nuclear forces and refuse to surrender without resort to those forces."

Kennedy argued that the United States should become more tolerant toward the Soviet Union, saying:

"No government or social system is so evil that its people must be considered as lacking in virtue. As Americans, we find communism profoundly repugnant [disgusting]… But we can still hail the Russian people for their many achievements."

He spoke of their common interests when he said:

"Among the many traits the peoples of our two countries have in common, none is stronger than our mutual abhorrence [hatred] of war… So let us not be blind to our differences—but let us also direct attention to our common interests and to the means by which those differences can be resolved."[20]

Read President Kennedy's speech here:

www.jfklibrary.org/Asset-Viewer/Archives/JFKPOF-045-002.aspx.

The legacy for Cuba

As a small country with a communist government, Cuba lived in fear of invasion. When the Soviet Union placed weapons there, the island had become a target. Now that the missiles had been withdrawn, Cuba remained vulnerable, despite U.S. promises not to invade. Since the Soviet Union had backed down in the face of U.S. pressure, Cuba could not rely on the Soviets to come to Cuba's rescue if the United States attacked it. Cubans suspected that the United States would be encouraged to invade Cuba.[21]

Castro learned that neither superpower could be trusted. Both countries had ignored Cuban views during the crisis—it appeared that the country was merely being used as a bargaining chip. In 1963, Castro realized just how true this was when he learned, during a visit to the Soviet Union, about the secret agreement of removing U.S. missiles in Turkey in exchange for withdrawing the Soviet ones in Cuba.[22]

The United States was the immediate threat. Castro had no faith in the U.S. guarantee not to invade Cuba. Yet he no longer trusted the Soviet Union to support him, either. As Castro explained

Could the United States and Cuba have come to an agreement?

The CIA continued its sabotage attacks against Cuba in an attempt to topple Castro, yet in the summer of 1963, the United States also tried to improve relations. In November of that year, President Kennedy made a speech noting that the only problem with Cuba was that it was encouraging revolution in other Latin American countries. Apart from this, it might be possible to come to some agreement. Castro thought Kennedy was sincere and might be able to coexist peacefully with Cuba. He even implied that he might have been able to do business with Kennedy after the 1964 election.

In the following quotation, Castro humorously suggests that if he said he was friendly with Kennedy's Republican opponent in the upcoming election, Barry Goldwater, Americans would react against Goldwater and vote for Kennedy:

"… He has come to understand many things over the past few months… I'm convinced that anyone else would be worse… You can tell him that I'm willing to declare Goldwater my friend if that will guarantee Kennedy's re-election."[26]

44

Cuba was too poor to afford good facilities. This class at a school in Cuba in 1963 was held outdoors. The desks and seats were made from raw wood by the students themselves.

to his Central Committee in 1968: "We realized how alone we would be in the event of a war."[23] Economic isolation also had serious effects. The Soviet Union continued to provide aid to Cuba, but the island still experienced economic problems because of the U.S. ban on trade, including a shortage of fuels and other basic necessities.

Fostering foreign relations

Understanding that it was unwise to rely on an alliance with the Soviet Union, Cuba worked to foster good relations with as many other countries in the world as possible, including non-communist countries.[24] The government also promoted revolution in other lands. It would be far easier for Cuba to survive if it could form alliances with other revolutionary governments. During the mid-1960s, Castro's government supported revolutionary movements in Latin American and African countries.[25]

A New Crisis: Vietnam

Although catastrophe had been averted in Cuba, the Cold War remained a significant factor in international politics. President Kennedy was faced with the threat of a large conflict in the small Southeast Asian country of Vietnam.

Vietnam and the Cold War

Vietnam won independence from French colonial rule in 1954. After the war, North Vietnam had a communist government, while South Vietnam was allied with the United States. The United States offered economic and military support to South Vietnam during the 1950s and early 1960s.

Early in his presidency, Kennedy saw Vietnam as crucial to the Cold War struggle. He believed it was essential to support South Vietnam to prevent the North Vietnamese communists from taking over and triggering a "domino" effect. He was determined to succeed in Vietnam after the failure of the Bay of Pigs invasion.

Civil conflict in South Vietnam

However, the South Vietnamese government was weak. President Ngo Dinh Diem, the ruler since 1955, refused to hold free elections, introduced harsh laws against opponents, and taxed the poor heavily. Opposition to Diem's government grew.

In 1960, the National Liberation Front for South Vietnam (NLF) was formed, including communist and non-communist opponents of the government.[1] Increasing numbers of people flocked to the NLF. Despite U.S. backing, Diem's army, the Army of the Republic of Vietnam (ARVN), was poorly trained and organized, and it experienced setbacks

The "domino theory"

Kennedy was a firm believer in the "domino theory." The outgoing U.S. president, Dwight D. Eisenhower, had warned Kennedy, "If we let South Vietnam fall, the next domino Laos, Cambodia, Burma, and on down the Subcontinent will fall."[3] There was evidence that communism could spread in this way. After World War II, the influence of the Soviet Union had grown in Eastern Europe, and communist governments had taken power in several countries, including East Germany, Hungary, and Poland. Kennedy therefore saw Vietnam as an important element in the Cold War struggle against the influence of the Soviet Union.

ARVN troops in action against the NLF in South Vietnam, 1961. They found it extremely difficult to root out guerrillas, and ultimately their mission would fail.

in its fight against the NLF. The United States feared that North Vietnam would invade the South, supported by the NLF.

In the fall of 1961, President Kennedy sent two key advisers—Walt Rostow and Maxwell Taylor—to Vietnam to assess the situation. They reported that Diem was losing the battle against the NLF. To bolster his government, they recommended sending military aid and U.S. advisers at all levels. Crucially, they suggested sending U.S. combat troops to Vietnam.[2]

General Maxwell Taylor 1901–1987

Born: Keytesville, Missouri

Role: U.S. army officer

General Maxwell Taylor had served in World War II and in the Korean War (1950–1953). During the Cuban Missile Crisis, he was the military representative of the U.S. president and a member of ExComm. Like the other members of the Joint Chiefs of Staff, he advocated taking a tough stance and invading Cuba. In 1962, President Kennedy appointed him the chairman of the Joint Chiefs of Staff. In 1964, Taylor became ambassador to South Vietnam. Under Kennedy and President Lyndon B. Johnson (served 1963–1969), Taylor pushed for strong conventional military forces to be used in limited wars, as an alternative to nuclear weapons.[4]

Did you know? In 1960, Taylor published a book, *The Uncertain Trumpet*, in which he criticized the United States' reliance on nuclear weapons.

Military advisers or troops?

President Kennedy was not eager to commit U.S. troops to Vietnam, but he chose to send military advisers, supplies, and aid to help the ARVN. The United States set up a command position in Saigon, the capital of South Vietnam, to run the assistance effort. The number of U.S. military personnel in Vietnam, less than 800 during the 1950s, rose to around 9,000 by mid-1962.[5]

With significant extra backing, the South Vietnamese army went on the offensive, but the NLF was still growing in power. In an attempt to prevent the further growth of the NLF, Diem's government introduced the Strategic Hamlet Program. Rural people were forced to move to new protected villages, where they were to be isolated from the influence of the NLF. This did not work. The villagers hated having to relocate, and it was impossible for the government to tell which villagers were in the NLF and which were not. Many NLF members lived within the villages, and others were recruited while there.[6]

Here, a U.S. military trainer shows a South Vietnamese soldier how to use a bayonet. The ARVN was also provided with a range of modern American weapons, including armored fighting vehicles and helicopter gunships.

NLF rises, Diem falls

By 1963, the NLF controlled territory containing up to half of the population of South Vietnam.[7] Here, life remained difficult, but the NLF introduced fairer policies than those offered by Diem's government. Taxes were based on people's ability to pay. It introduced moderate land reform, distributing some land owned by the biggest landlords.

Opposition to Diem's government continued to grow. From May 1963, Buddhists (people following the religion of Buddhism) organized strikes and demonstrations to protest the discrimination they suffered under Diem, who favored Roman Catholics. Students and the professional classes joined the movement.

By the summer, the United States doubted that Diem could defeat the NLF. On November 2, Diem was toppled, with U.S. support, and South Vietnamese army officers assassinated him. We will never know how Kennedy would have dealt with the new government, because just three weeks later, on November 22, Kennedy himself was assassinated in Dallas, Texas.

What do you think?:

Would Kennedy have gotten out of Vietnam?

If he had not been assassinated, would President Kennedy have become more embroiled in Vietnam, or would he have resolved the issues? It is unclear how he would have proceeded. Kennedy's legacy in Vietnam in 1962 has been summed up as: "indecision, half-measures, and gradually increasing involvement."[8]

Perhaps he would have introduced U.S. troops, as Walt Rostow and Maxwell Taylor recommended. However, some historians argue that he would have managed to keep the United States out of Vietnam. Kennedy had shown that he was capable of standing up to the military. Through his successful handling of the Cuban Missile Crisis, he had demonstrated that he was capable of defending the United States' interests without resorting to direct military intervention. There is evidence that he planned to reduce the number of U.S. military personnel in Vietnam.[9] Could he have solved the issues using diplomacy backed by military threat, as he had in Cuba? If so, the history of Vietnam would have been very different.

An Overview

How else could the Cuban Missile Crisis have turned out? If Khrushchev had not backed down in time, would President Kennedy have listened to his Joint Chiefs of Staff and launched air strikes and an invasion? The United States had intervened in many other Latin American countries in the past (including Cuba from 1917 to 1933) to further its own interests.[1] In a later interview, Robert McNamara said that he believed that if the United States had attacked Cuba, the Soviet Union would have responded with a counterattack somewhere else in the world—perhaps against Berlin or the U.S. missiles in Turkey.[2]

Might President Kennedy have used nuclear weapons against Cuba? Secretary of State Dean Rusk had alluded to the possibility of "eliminating" Cuba (see page 25). The United States was the only country to have already used nuclear bombs, to devastating effect (see page 4). If the United States had initiated a nuclear strike on Cuba, it would have destroyed the entire island and its people. Would the Soviet Union have responded by firing on the United States? It is doubtful, as the evidence indicates that the Soviet Union was not wholly committed to Cuba.

Kennedy's push for peace

However, it is extremely unlikely that President Kennedy would have

The aftermath of the nuclear attack on Hiroshima in August 1945, which destroyed most of the city and killed at least 70,000 people outright or shortly after the blast.

unleashed nuclear weapons on Cuba. Evidence revealed in 1987 about the events during the Cuban Missile Crisis indicates that Kennedy was prepared to go further for peace. If necessary, he would have publicly agreed to withdraw the missiles from Turkey in exchange for removing the missiles from Cuba.[3] Khrushchev did not know this at the time. This evidence shows that Kennedy was determined to avoid a war that could have left millions dead.

Concerning relations with Cuba, if Kennedy had lived, might he have come to a peaceful understanding with Cuba? He made attempts to improve relations with Cuba, and Castro himself said he might be able to do business with Kennedy after the 1964 election (see page 44).

A broader question concerns the Cold War in general. Might Kennedy have been able to ease the tensions with the Soviet Union? It is extraordinarily difficult to judge how the actions of one person, no matter how powerful, could have influenced international relations.

The end of the Cold War

The Cold War continued for three more decades. After the Soviet Union invaded Afghanistan in 1979, tensions between the superpowers rose again, and there were renewed fears of nuclear conflict.

However, during the mid-1980s, the Soviet system began to collapse, and tensions with the West gradually eased. Starting in 1989, Eastern European countries toppled their communist rulers. In 1991, the Soviet Union itself fell apart, and the countries within it formed independent states, including Ukraine, Belarus, Kazakhstan, and Russia.

What do you think?:

Could the crisis have been prevented?

Some historians blame President Kennedy for allowing the missile crisis to develop in the first place. He had launched the Bay of Pigs invasion, which had made an enemy of Cuba and led it to seek the Soviet Union for help with its defense. The Soviet Union took advantage of this to base missiles in Cuba. Could this have been avoided if Kennedy had decided against the invasion? On the other hand, would ignoring Cuba have allowed communism to spread more easily in Latin America?

The legacy of John F. Kennedy

What are the most significant legacies of John F. Kennedy's short but eventful presidency?

At home

In terms of his domestic policy, President Kennedy was criticized for being slow to appreciate the importance of the civil rights movement.[4] It was only after the confrontations over segregation in Mississippi and Alabama (see page 12) that he finally committed himself in June 1963 to putting a civil rights bill before Congress. However, all the major initiatives became law under the next president, Lyndon B. Johnson, so it could be argued that Kennedy laid the foundations for these reforms.[5]

A clearer legacy of Kennedy's presidency is the Peace Corps, which is still running successfully in the early 21st century. His space program also came to fruition, when Neil Armstrong set foot on the Moon in 1969.

In the world

During the Bay of Pigs invasion, the U.S. government attempted to interfere in the internal affairs of another country. After the failure of the operation, no U.S. government ever invaded Cuba again. However, U.S. governments intervened in many other countries to promote governments favorable to their interests. Thus, the tradition of U.S. military involvement in the affairs of other countries was unchanged by President Kennedy.

This disarmed Soviet missile is now on public display in Havana, Cuba. It is part of an exhibit remembering the Cuban Missile Crisis.

The Cuban Missile Crisis

Were the decisions that President Kennedy made during the Cuban Missile Crisis the most important of his career? It has been argued that Kennedy bore some

After a democratic revolution in the Dominican Republic in 1965, the United States feared it would become communist, so it occupied the country. Here, U.S. Marines search a suspected opponent, 1965.

responsibility for creating the crisis because he chose to take actions that antagonized Cuba and the Soviet Union:

• He launched the Bay of Pigs invasion.

• He ordered undercover action against Cuba and Castro.

• He continued the massive buildup of U.S. nuclear weapons.

• He placed intermediate-range ballistic missiles in Turkey.[6]

Yet many historians agree that the decisions President Kennedy made during the crucial days of October 1962 were the most important of his presidency. This climax of Cold War tensions between the United States and the Soviet Union was the closest the world has ever come to nuclear war.[7] According to historian Robert Dallek, considering Kennedy's legacy of nearly 1,000 days in office, "October 1962 was not only Kennedy's finest hour in the White House; it was also an imperishable [long-lasting] example of how one man prevented a catastrophe that may yet afflict the world."[8]

Limited Test Ban Treaty

President Kennedy did signal a change by initiating the Limited Test Ban Treaty (see page 42). Some historians contend that this treaty was one of Kennedy's most significant achievements. According to historian Robert Dallek:

"The treaty—the first significant arms control agreement between the United States and USSR [Soviet Union]—was a milestone in the successful forty-five-year struggle to prevent the Cold War from turning into an all-out conflict that would have devastated the planet."[9]

Timeline

1917	1940	1943	1946	1952	1959
May 29 John F. Kennedy is born in Brookline, Massachusetts	**July** Kennedy publishes his first book, *Why England Slept*	**August** During World War II, Kennedy leads his men to safety after a Japanese destroyer attacks their boat	**November 5** Kennedy is elected to the House of Representatives and serves three terms	**November 4** Kennedy is elected to the Senate	**January 1** In Cuba, Fidel Castro's forces topple Fulgencio Batista. Civil war rages in Laos

1961	1961	1961	1961	1961
December 2 Castro declares himself a communist	**October** Kennedy sends two senior advisers to Vietnam to assess the situation there	**August 12–13** Khrushchev's forces build a wall between East and West Berlin to divide Soviet-ruled East Berlin from Western-ruled West Berlin	**July 25** In a speech, Kennedy says he will not allow the Soviet Union to drive Western forces out of Berlin, but that he is willing to negotiate	**June 3–4** Kennedy attends the Vienna summit, where he talks to Soviet leader Khrushchev about ending nuclear weapons testing and a strategy for the divided city of Berlin

1962	1962	1962	1962	1962
July Cuban Minister of the Armed Forces Raúl Castro visits Moscow, in the Soviet Union, to seek military support	**August 29** The crew of U.S. spy planes notice military building projects and Soviet technicians in Cuba	**October 14** A U.S. spy plane takes photos over Cuba that give evidence of offensive weapons	**October 16** Kennedy forms an advisory team, ExComm, to discuss the missile crisis in Cuba	**October 17** ExComm meets to discuss the options for tackling the crisis

1962	1962	1962
December 29 Kennedy speaks to Cuban exiles and promises that the U.S. government will continue to work to topple Castro. In Laos, an agreement states that the government will become neutral: left-wing, neutral, and right-wing politicians will share power in the government. *By the end of the year* The U.S. government increases the number of military advisers in Vietnam to 15,000	**November 20** Kennedy's government calls for a law to stop racial segregation in public housing	**November 6** In elections for the U.S. Congress, the Democrats win more seats, increasing their majority

1963	1963	1963
June 10 Kennedy makes a "peace speech," calling for a more sympathetic attitude toward the Soviet Union	**June 19** Kennedy asks Congress for support to pass civil rights laws to integrate public facilities	**August 5** The United States, Soviet Union, and Great Britain sign a treaty in Moscow, agreeing in principle to ban the testing of nuclear weapons

1960
July 5
The new Cuban government takes over all U.S. property in Cuba

1960
July 6
The United States stops buying sugar from Cuba

1960
August 7
Cuba takes over all large U.S.-owned industrial and agrarian (farm) businesses

1960
October
The U.S. government stops most exports to Cuba

1960
November 8
Kennedy is elected president of the United States

1961
January 3
U.S. President Dwight D. Eisenhower breaks diplomatic ties with Cuba

1961
May 25
Kennedy declares a commitment for the United States to land a man on the Moon by the end of the 1960s

1961
May
There is a ceasefire in the civil war in Laos

1961
April 15
Kennedy allows the Bay of Pigs invasion of Cuba to go ahead. Exiled Cuban pilots bomb Cuban airbases and invade Cuba, but they are defeated.

1961
March 1
Kennedy sets up the Peace Corps, which sends young Americans to developing countries to contribute their skills there

1961
January 20
Kennedy is sworn in as president

1962
October 20
Kennedy proclaims his "quarantine" plan to blockade Soviet ships, to prevent them from reaching Cuba

1962
October 22
Kennedy addresses the nation on television to make the crisis public, and he demands that the Soviet Union remove the missiles from Cuba. He writes a letter to Khrushchev with the same message.

1962
October 23
Khrushchev replies to Kennedy, saying that the missiles are purely defensive

1962
October 24
The U.S. Navy activates the quarantine policy; most Soviet ships turn back

1962
October 25
There is a confrontation between U.S. and Soviet representatives at the United Nations

1962
October 29
An agreement between the United States and the Soviet Union is reached, and the crisis is over

1962
October 28
Khrushchev agrees to remove the missiles. He accepts a secret promise from Kennedy to remove the missiles in Turkey within four to five months.

1962
October 27
Khrushchev sends a second letter saying that US missiles should be removed from Turkey. Rather than initiate a military attack on Cuba, Kennedy replies to Khrushchev's first letter, accepting the suggested deal

1962
October 26
Khrushchev sends a letter to Kennedy proposing a deal: he would remove the missiles if Kennedy agrees not to invade Cuba.

1963
August 28
More than 250,000 civil rights protesters, led by Martin Luther King, Jr., march on Washington, D.C.

1963
November 18
Kennedy makes a speech implying that it might be possible to come to some agreement with Castro; Castro responds positively

1963
November 22
Kennedy is assassinated in Dallas, Texas

1987
It is revealed that Kennedy would have gone further to avoid war in the Cuban Missile Crisis: he would have publicly agreed to remove missiles from Turkey

Notes on Sources

On the Brink of Nuclear War (pages 4–5)

1. *Encyclopaedia Britannica*, "World War II," http://library.eb.co.uk/eb/article-53605?query=hiroshima&ct=.

2. Learners Online, "Revisiting the Cuban Missile Crisis," http://www.learnersonline.com/weekly/lessons02/week39/index.htm/.

3. h2g2, "The Cuban Missile Crisis," http://h2g2.com/approved_entry/A563852.

4. National Archives, "Extracts from a United States Information Booklet on the Situation in Cuba," October 29, 1962, http://www.nationalarchives.gov.uk/education/heroesvillains/pdf/g2cs2s4.pdf.

The Making of a President (pages 6–13)

1. *Encyclopaedia Britannica*, "John F. Kennedy," http://library.eb.co.uk/eb/article-3866.

2. *Ibid.*

3. Howard S. Kaplan, *John F. Kennedy: A Photographic Story of a Life* (London: Dorling Kindersley, 2005), 39.

4. *Ibid.*, 44–46.

5. *Ibid.*, 50.

6. *Ibid.*, 52.

7. *Ibid.*, 53.

8. The Library of Congress, "A Century of Racial Segregation, 1849–1950," http://www.loc.gov/exhibits/brown/brown-segregation.html.

9. *Encyclopaedia Britannica*, "John F. Kennedy."

10. Betty Boyd Caroli, "Jacqueline Kennedy Onassis," *Encyclopaedia Britannica*, http://www.britannica.com/EBchecked/topic/428919/Jacqueline-Kennedy-Onassis.

11. Kaplan, *John F. Kennedy: A Photographic Story of a Life*, 81.

12. *Ibid.*; and *Encyclopaedia Britannica*, "John F. Kennedy."

13. John F. Kennedy, "'Ask not what your country can do for you,'" *The Guardian*, http://www.guardian.co.uk/theguardian/2007/apr/22/greatspeeches.

14. *Encyclopaedia Britannica*, "James Meredith," http://www.britannica.com/EBchecked/topic/375972/James-Meredith.

15. Robert Dallek, *John F. Kennedy: An Unfinished Life, 1917–1963* (London: Penguin, 2003), 594.

16. *Ibid.*, 604.

17. *Ibid.*, 643.

18. *Ibid.*, 603.

19. *Ibid.*, 590.

20. Robert R. Gilruth, "I Believe We Should Go to the Moon," NASA, http://history.nasa.gov/SP-350/ch-2-1.html.

21. *Encyclopaedia Britannica*, "Peace Corps," http://library.eb.co.uk/eb/article-9058852?query=Peace%20Corps&ct=.

The United States and the World, 1961–1962 (pages 14–21)

1. Leslie Bethell, *Cuba: A Short History* (Cambridge: Cambridge University Press, 1993), 96.

2. *Encyclopaedia Britannica*, "Fidel Castro," http://library.eb.co.uk/eb/article-9020736?query=fidel%20castro&ct=.

3. *Encyclopaedia Britannica*, "Raúl Castro," http://library.eb.co.uk/eb/article-9439238?query=raul%20castro&ct=null.

4. Bethell, *Cuba: A Short History*, 19.

5. *Ibid.*, 99.

6. Richard Gott, *Cuba: A New History* (New Haven: Yale University Press, 2005), 194.

7. *Ibid.*, 190.

8. *Ibid.*, 194.

9. Dallek, *John F. Kennedy: An Unfinished Life*, 368.

10. PBS, "Operation Mongoose: The Covert Operation to Remove Castro from Power," http://www.pbs.org/wgbh/amex/rfk/peopleevents/e_mongoose.html.

11. Global Security, "Operation Mongoose," http://www.globalsecurity.org/intell/ops/mongoose.htm.

12. Gott, *Cuba: A New History*, 208–209.

13. *Ibid.*, 217.

14. Lawrence Freedman, *Kennedy's Wars: Berlin, Cuba, Laos, and Vietnam* (Oxford: Oxford University Press, 2000), 60.

15. *Ibid.*, 68–69.

16. *Ibid.*, 71.

17. *Ibid.*, 112.

18. The Papers of George Washington, "Washington's First Annual Message to Congress," http://gwpapers.virginia.edu/documents/union/state1.html.

19. John F. Kennedy Presidential Library and Museum, "Radio and Television Report to the American People on the Berlin Crisis, July 25, 1961," http://www.jfklibrary.org/Research/Ready-Reference/JFK-Speeches/Radio-and-Television-Report-to-the-American-People-on-the-Berlin-Crisis-July-25-1961.aspx/.

20. Dallek, *John F. Kennedy: An Unfinished Life*, 305.

21. Freedman, *Kennedy's Wars*, 294.

22. *Ibid.*, 295.

23. *Ibid.*, 296.

24. *Ibid.*, 299.

25. Dallek, *John F. Kennedy: An Unfinished Life*, 353.

26. Freedman, *Kennedy's Wars*, 298.

27. *Ibid.*, 300.

The Cuban Missile Crisis Develops (pages 22–29)

1. Dallek, *John F. Kennedy: An Unfinished Life*, 536.

2. Library of Congress, "Revelations from the Russian Archives: The Cuban Missile Crisis," July 22, 2010, http://www.loc.gov/exhibits/archives/colc.html.

3. Dallek, *John F. Kennedy: An Unfinished Life*, 536.

4. Natural Resources Defense Council, "Table of Global Nuclear Weapons Stockpiles, 1945–2002," November 25, 2002, http://www.nrdc.org/nuclear/nudb/datab19.asp.

5. Ernest R. May, "John F. Kennedy and the Cuban Missile Crisis," BBC History, http://www.bbc.co.uk/history/worldwars/coldwar/kennedy_cuban_missile_01.shtml.

6. Gott, *Cuba: A New History*, 201.

7. Dallek, *John F. Kennedy: An Unfinished Life*, 539.

8. History Learning Site, "The Cuban Missile Crisis," http://www.historylearningsite.co.uk/cuban_missile_crisis.htm.

9. *Encyclopaedia Britannica*, "Nikita Sergeyevich Khrushchev," http://library.eb.co.uk/eb/article-3903.

10. Yale Law School, The Avalon Project, "Cuban Missile Crisis: Transcript of a Meeting at the White House, October 16, 1962," http://avalon.law.yale.edu/20th_century/msc_cuba018.asp.

11. Dallek, *John F. Kennedy: An Unfinished Life*, 552.

12. History Learning Site, "The Cuban Missile Crisis"; and Spartacus Educational Publishers, "Cuban Missile Crisis," http://www.spartacus.schoolnet.co.uk/COLDcubanmissile.htm.

13. U.S. Department of Defense, "Robert S. McNamara," http://www.defense.gov/specials/secdef_histories/bios/mcnamara.htm.

14. ThinkQuest, "Robert McNamara," http://library.thinkquest.org/11046/people/r_mcnamara.html.

15. ThinkQuest, "The Situation Room," http://library.thinkquest.org/11046/sitroom/index.html?tqskip1=1&tqtime=1012.

16. ThinkQuest, "The Situation Room."

17. Nathaniel Harris, *The Cuban Missile Crisis* (London: Hodder Wayland, 2002), 6.

18. Gott, *Cuba: A New History*, 205.

19. National Archives, "Kennedy & Cuba: Why Didn't This Lead to Nuclear War?" http://www.nationalarchives.gov.uk/education/heroesvillains/pdf/g2cs2s2.pdf.

20. Harris, *The Cuban Missile Crisis*, 16.

Blockade! (pages 30–35)

1. Harris, *The Cuban Missile Crisis*, 16.

2. Department of History Inside the Oval Office, "How Close?: Cuban Missiles and the End of the World," February 20, 2008, http://www.cas.sc.edu/hist/ovalofficetapes/cuban%20missile%20crisis.htm.

3. Harris, *The Cuban Missile Crisis*, 14.

4. Dallek, *John F. Kennedy: An Unfinished Life*, 563.

5. Gott, *Cuba: A New History*, 206.

6. *Ibid.*

7. Harris, *The Cuban Missile Crisis*, 14.

8. *Ibid.*

9. *Ibid.*

10. Freedman, *Kennedy's Wars*, 204.

11. Global Security, "Cuban Missile Crisis," http://www.globalsecurity.org/military/ops/cuba-62.htm.

12. United States History, "Cuban Missile Crisis," http://www.u-s-history.com/pages/h1736.html.

13. ThinkQuest, "Robert Kennedy," http://library.thinkquest.org/11046/people/r_kennedy.html.

14. Russian Foreign Ministry Archives, "Dobryin Cable to the USSR Foreign Ministry," October 27, 1962, http://www.gwu.edu/~nsarchiv/nsa/cuba_mis_cri/621027%20Dobrynin%20Cable%20to%20USSR.pdf.

15. ThinkQuest, "Robert Kennedy."

16. National Archives, "Extracts from Khrushchev's letter to Kennedy, 26 October 1962," http://www.nationalarchives.gov.uk/education/heroesvillains/pdf/g2cs2s6.pdf.

Resolution and Aftermath (pages 36–45)

1. Dallek, *John F. Kennedy: An Unfinished Life*, 567–68.

2. Learners Online, "Revisiting the Cuban Missile Crisis."

3. Dallek, *John F. Kennedy: An Unfinished Life*, 568.

4. *Ibid.*, 569.

5. Dallek, *John F. Kennedy: An Unfinished Life*, 569.

6. *Ibid.*, 570.

7. Gott, *Cuba: A New History*, 207.

8. Harris, *The Cuban Missile Crisis*, 26.

9. *Ibid.*, 27.

10. *Ibid.*, 24.

11. National Security Archive, "Interview with Robert McNamara," December 13, 1998, http:// www.gwu.edu/~nsarchiv/coldwar/interviews/episode-10/mcnamara1.html.

12. Gott, *Cuba: A New History*, 207.

13. *Ibid.*, 208.

14. *Encyclopaedia Britannica*, "Guantánamo Bay," http://library.eb.co.uk/eb/article-9038306?query=guantanamo&ct=null.

15. Department of the Navy, Naval History and Heritage Command, "Cuban Missile Crisis, 1962," August 28, 2006, http://www.history.navy.mil/faqs/faq90-1.htm; from Curtis Utz, *Cordon of Steel: The U.S. Navy and the Cuban Missile Crisis* (Washington, D.C.: Naval Historical Center, 1993), 1.

16. Dallek, *John F. Kennedy: An Unfinished Life*, 572.

17. *Ibid.*, 572.

18. *Ibid.*, 630.

19. *Ibid.*, 619.

20. *Ibid.*, 621.

21. James G. Blight and Philip Brenner, "Lessons of Cuban Missile Crisis," in *Sad and Luminous Days: Cuba's Secret Struggles with the Superpowers after the Cuban Missile Crisis* (Lanham, Md.: Rowman & Littlefield Publishing Group), http://www.historyofcuba.com/history/Sad-1.htm.

22. *Ibid.*

23. *Ibid.*

24. Bethell, *Cuba: A Short History*, 139.

25. *Ibid.*, 139–40.

26. Freedman, *Kennedy's Wars*, 243.

A New Crisis: Vietnam (pages 46–49)

1. Cath Senker, *Living Through the Vietnam War* (Chicago: Raintree, 2012), 12.

2. *Encyclopaedia Britannica*, "Vietnam War: The U.S. Role Grows," http://library.eb.co.uk/eb/article-234631.

3. Michael Maclear, *The Ten Thousand Day War* (London: Thames Mandarin, 1989), 79.

4. "Maxwell Davenport Taylor," in *Merriam-Webster's Biographical Dictionary* (Springfield, Mass.: Merriam-Webster, 1995), 1011.

5. *Encyclopaedia Britannica*, "Vietnam War: The U.S. Role Grows."

6. *Encyclopaedia Britannica*, "Vietnam War: The Conflict Deepens," http://library.eb.co.uk/eb/article-234632.

7. Senker, *Living Through the Vietnam War*, 15.

8. *Encyclopaedia Britannica*, "Vietnam War: The Conflict Deepens."

9. Dallek, *John F. Kennedy: An Unfinished Life*, 710.

An Overview (pages 50–53)

1. Mark Becker, "History of U.S. Interventions in Latin America," Marc's House of Knowledge, http://www.yachana.org/teaching//resources/interventions.html.

2. National Security Archive, "Interview with Robert McNamara."

3. Dallek, *John F. Kennedy: An Unfinished Life*, 569.

4. *Ibid.*, 707.

5. *Ibid.*, 708.

6. Barton J. Bernstein, cited in Dallek, *John F. Kennedy: An Unfinished Life*, 573.

7. Thomas Blanton, "Annals of Blinkmanship [sic]," The National Security Archive, summer 1997, http://www.gwu.edu/~nsarchiv/nsa/cuba_mis_cri/annals.htm.

8. *Ibid.*

9. Dallek, *John F. Kennedy: An Unfinished Life*, 630.

Glossary

ally country that has agreed to help and support another country, especially in case of a war

ambassador senior official living in another country as the representative of his or her own country

arms weapons, especially as used by a country's army, navy, or air force

assassinate murder a famous person for political reasons

back channel in diplomacy, informal discussions held by governments and leaders about sensitive political issues

ballistic missile long-range missile fired high into the sky that curves down to strike its target

blockade stop goods from entering or leaving a place

capitalism economic system under which private owners rather than the government run a country's businesses and industry for profit

Central Intelligence Agency (CIA) department of the U.S. government that collects information about other countries, often secretly, and makes plans to intervene in other countries to defend U.S. interests

civil right right to be treated equally, no matter a person's background, race, color, and so on

civil war war between groups of people living in the same country

Cold War hostile relations between the Western powers (led by the United States) and countries linked to the Soviet Union, from 1949 to 1990

communism system of government in the former Soviet Union and elsewhere in which the government control the production of goods and the running of services

communist person or country that follows the ideas of communism

conventional non-nuclear weapon or force, such as a tank or warship

democracy system of government in which all the adults of a country can vote to elect their representatives

Democrat supporter of the Democratic Party of the United States, which tends to support reform to help poorer members of society and favors government involvement in the running of the economy

diplomacy managing of relations between different countries; also refers to the skill in doing this

diplomatic related to the managing of relations between countries; when diplomatic relations are broken off, the countries no longer have representatives talking officially to each other

discrimination treating a particular group in society unfairly

domestic referring to policies, the ones that are carried out within a particular country

exile living in a country other than the one where you were born, usually for political reasons

federal in the U.S., relating to the national government rather than the government of an individual state

guerrilla fighter against a regular army

impasse difficult situation in which it is impossible to make progress because the people involved cannot agree what to do

integrate allow people from different backgrounds to live or work together or to use the same public facilities

Joint Chiefs of Staff in the U.S., leaders of the armed forces advising the president on military matters

legacy situation that exists because of actions that took place in the past

legislation law passed by the government

Nazi member of the National Socialist party that ruled Germany from 1933 to 1945

New Frontier phrase John F. Kennedy used to describe his policies and vision for the country, which involved asking all Americans to join together to create new achievements in society, science, and space

nuclear to do with weapons that use nuclear energy

offensive weapon weapon with the purpose of attacking someone

quarantine usually means keeping people away from others to prevent the spread of disease; in the context in which Kennedy used the word during the Cuban Missile Crisis, it meant "blockade"

regime government, especially one that was not elected in a fair way

Republican in the U.S., supporter of the Republican Party, generally favoring less government intervention in society and the economy

reservist in the army, member of the reserves, a force of trained but part-time soldiers who can be used in an emergency

retaliation action people or countries take against a person or country that has harmed them

revolution complete change in the government of a country, often achieved by violent action

sabotage causing deliberate damage to buildings, equipment, or transportation for a political reason

segregation separating people of different races and treating them differently

social security system in which people pay money regularly to the government when they are working and receive payments from the government when they are unable to work, especially when they are sick or too old to work

Soviet relating to the Soviet Union

Soviet Union former empire, ruled from Moscow in Russia, stretching from the Baltic and Black Seas to the Pacific Ocean, from 1922 to 1991

subversion to try to destroy the authority, for example, of a government, by attacking it secretly or indirectly

summit official meeting between the leaders of two or more governments at which they discuss important matters

superpower country that has great economic power and global influence

thesis long work written by a student based on his or her own research

torpedo narrow weapon that travels underwater to strike and explode against its target

Find Out More

Books

Nonfiction

Anderson, Catherine Corley. *John F. Kennedy* (Just the Facts Biographies). Minneapolis: Lerner, 2006.

Edison, Erin. *John F. Kennedy* (Presidential Biographies). Mankato, Minn.: Capstone, 2013.

Immell, Myra. *The Cuban Missile Crisis* (Perspectives on Modern World History). Detroit: Greenhaven, 2011.

Sandler, Martin W. *Kennedy Through the Lens*. New York: Walker, 2011.

Stein, R. Conrad. Cuban Missile Crisis: *In the Shadow of Nuclear War* (America's Living History). Berkeley Heights, N.J.: Enslow, 2009.

Wagner, Heather Lehr. *The Cuban Missile Crisis: Cold War Confrontation* (Milestones in American History). New York: Chelsea House, 2011.

Fiction

Almond, David. *The Fire-eaters*. New York: Delacorte, 2004. This book tells the story of a boy growing up in the United States at a time when the United States and Soviet Union were testing nuclear missiles.

DVD

The Fog of War (Columbia TriStar Home Entertainment, 2004)
In this documentary, Robert McNamara, secretary of defense in the Kennedy and Johnson administrations, discusses the U.S. commitment to the Vietnam War.

Thirteen Days (New Line Home Entertainment, 2001)
This political thriller is about the Cuban Missile Crisis from the U.S. government's perspective.

Web sites

www.biography.com/people/john-f-kennedy-9362930
Find out more about John F. Kennedy at this site.

www.gwu.edu/~nsarchiv/nsa/cuba_mis_cri/
The National Security Archive offers information about the Cuban Missile Crisis, including formerly secret documents from U.S., Cuban, Soviet, and Eastern European archives.

www.jfklibrary.org/JFK/JFK-in-History/Cuban-Missile-Crisis.aspx
Visit the web site of the John F. Kennedy Presidential Library and Museum to learn more about the president and about the Cuban Missile Crisis.

library.thinkquest.org/11046
This ThinkQuest web site is aimed at students, with details of the Cuban Missile Crisis and the major players involved.

Other topics to research

You might like to find out more about the Cold War and the relationship between the United States and the Soviet Union. You could also look into the wars caused by the clash between communist and non-communist powers, such as in Vietnam. Perhaps you could compare the decisions made by President Lyndon B. Johnson in Vietnam with those made by Kennedy during his presidency. You could also look into the U.S. naval base at Guantánamo Bay.

Index